United States Government Accountability Office

Report to Congressional Requesters

March 2012

PIPELINE SAFETY

Collecting Data and Sharing Information on Federally Unregulated Gathering Pipelines Could Help Enhance Safety

March 2012

PIPELINE SAFETY

Collecting Data and Sharing Information on Federally Unregulated Gathering Pipelines Could Help Enhance Safety

Why GAO Did This Study

Pipelines are a relatively safe mode of transportation for hazardous liquid and natural gas and are regulated by the Department of Transportation's (DOT) Pipeline and Hazardous Materials Safety Administration (PHMSA) and state entities. Included in the nation's pipeline network are an estimated 200,000 or more miles of onshore "gathering" pipelines, which transport products to processing facilities and larger pipelines. (See figure.) Many of these pipelines have not been subject to federal regulation based on their generally rural location and low operating pressures. While incidents involving gathering pipelines regulated by PHMSA have resulted in millions of dollars in property damage in recent years, comparable statistics for federally unregulated gathering pipelines are unknown. This report identifies (1) the safety risks that exist, if any, with onshore hazardous liquid and natural gas gathering pipelines that are not currently under PHMSA regulation and (2) the practices states use to help ensure the safety of these pipelines. GAO surveyed state pipeline safety agencies in all 50 states and the District of Columbia; interviewed officials at PHMSA, state pipeline safety agencies, pipeline companies, and industry associations; and analyzed data and regulations.

What GAO Recommends

DOT should (1) collect data on federally unregulated hazardous liquid and gas gathering pipelines and (2) establish an online clearinghouse or other resource for sharing information on pipeline safety practices. DOT provided technical corrections on a draft of this report.

View GAO-12-388. For more information, contact Susan A. Fleming at (202) 512-2834 or flemings@gao.gov.

What GAO Found

While the safety risks of onshore gathering pipelines that are not regulated by PHMSA are generally considered to be lower than for other types of pipelines, PHMSA does not collect comprehensive data to identify the safety risks of unregulated gathering pipelines. In response to a GAO survey, state pipeline safety agencies cited construction quality, maintenance practices, unknown or uncertain locations, and limited or no information on pipeline integrity as among the highest risks for federally unregulated pipelines. Without data on these risk factors, pipeline safety officials are unable to assess and manage safety risks associated with these pipelines. Furthermore, changes in pipeline operational environments cited in response to GAO's survey and by industry officials could also increase safety risks for federally unregulated gathering pipelines. Specifically, land-use changes are resulting in development encroaching on existing pipelines and the increased extraction of oil and natural gas from shale deposits is resulting in the development of new gathering pipelines, some of which are larger in diameter and operate at higher pressure than older pipelines. PHMSA is considering collecting data on federally unregulated gathering pipelines, but the agency's plans are preliminary, and the extent to which PHMSA will collect data sufficient to evaluate the potential safety risks associated with these pipelines is uncertain.

A small number of state pipeline safety agencies GAO surveyed reported using at least one of five practices that were most frequently cited to help ensure the safety of federally unregulated pipelines. These practices include (1) damage prevention programs, (2) considering areas of highest risk to target resources, (3) safety inspections, (4) public outreach and communication, and (5) increased regulatory attention on operators with prior spills or leaks. However, the sharing of information among states on the safety practices used appears to be limited. Some state and PHMSA officials GAO interviewed had limited awareness of safety practices used by other states. Increased communication and information sharing about pipeline safety practices could boost the use of such practices for unregulated pipelines. However, information targeted at gathering pipelines on PHMSA's website, including relevant safety practices and state activities, is limited.

Pipeline System

Wellheads — Gathering pipelines — Processing facility — Transmission pipeline — Distribution pipelines — Meters

Source: PHMSA.

_____ United States Government Accountability Office

Contents

Abbreviations

ANPRM	Advanced Notice of Proposed Rulemaking
DOT	Department of Transportation
NAPSR	National Association of Pipeline Safety Representatives
PHMSA	Pipeline and Hazardous Materials Safety Administration
psi	pounds per square inch

United States Government Accountability Office
Washington, DC 20548

March 22, 2012

The Honorable John D. Rockefeller IV
Chairman
Committee on Commerce, Science,
   and Transportation
United States Senate

The Honorable Frank R. Lautenberg
Chairman
Subcommittee on Surface Transportation
   and Merchant Marine Infrastructure,
   Safety, and Security
Committee on Commerce, Science, and Transportation
United States Senate

Pipelines are a relatively safe mode of transportation for hazardous liquid and natural gas. The nation's network of more than 2.5 million miles of pipeline is largely regulated by the Department of Transportation's (DOT) Pipeline and Hazardous Materials Safety Administration (PHMSA) and state entities. Part of this network consists of more than 200,000 miles (estimated) of onshore "gathering" pipelines, which transport hazardous liquid and natural gas products from wells to processing facilities and to larger transmission pipelines. Many of these gathering pipelines, however, have not been subject to PHMSA regulation because they are generally located away from population centers and operate at low pressures.[1] In recent years, incidents involving gathering pipelines regulated by PHMSA have resulted in millions of dollars in property damage. Comparable statistics for federally unregulated gathering pipelines are unknown because PHMSA does not collect such data.

You requested that we review pipeline safety issues related to onshore gathering pipelines not regulated by PHMSA. To do so, we examined (1) the safety risks that exist, if any, with onshore hazardous liquid and natural gas gathering pipelines that are not currently under PHMSA

---

[1]PHMSA has limited statutory authority to regulate such pipelines under 49 U.S.C. § 60101(b).

         GAO-12-388 Pipeline Safety

regulation and (2) the practices states use to help ensure the safety of these federally unregulated onshore gathering pipelines.

To identify safety risks that may be associated with gathering pipelines, we reviewed PHMSA safety regulations and analyzed data on pipelines regulated by PHMSA to understand the types of pipeline data currently collected, as well as to compare and analyze accident, injury, fatality, and other trends. We determined that these data were complete, reasonable, and sufficiently reliable for the purposes of this report. For both objectives, we developed and administered a survey to 52 pipeline safety agencies[2] in all 50 states and the District of Columbia to collect information on, among other things, onshore gathering pipelines, the perceived pipeline safety risks associated with those pipelines, and the safety practices used for those pipelines. We received a 100 percent response rate for this survey. We also interviewed officials at PHMSA, selected state pipeline safety agencies, pipeline companies, and industry associations. We conducted site visits to Dallas-Fort Worth, Denver, and Pittsburgh; we selected these locations based on geography, existing pipeline infrastructure, and other factors.

We conducted this performance audit from February 2011 to March 2012 in accordance with generally accepted government auditing standards. Those standards require that we plan and perform the audit to obtain sufficient, appropriate evidence to provide a reasonable basis for our findings and conclusions based on our audit objectives. We believe that the evidence obtained provides a reasonable basis for our findings and conclusions based on our audit objectives.

Background

Pipelines transport roughly two-thirds of domestic energy supplies through approximately 2.5 million miles of pipelines throughout the United States. These pipelines carry hazardous liquids and natural gas from producing wells to end users (residences and businesses). Within this nationwide system, there are three main types of pipelines.

---

[2]Two state pipeline safety officials from separate agencies in Arkansas that are responsible for overseeing pipeline safety in that state responded to our survey. Also, Alaska and Hawaii have chosen not to participate in pipeline arrangements with PHMSA. Therefore, a PHMSA official who conducts state pipeline safety inspections in these states responded to those states' surveys.

- *Gathering pipelines.* Gas gathering pipelines collect natural gas from production areas, while hazardous liquid gathering pipelines collect oil and other petroleum products. These pipelines then typically transport the products to processing facilities, which in turn refine and send the products to transmission pipelines. According to PHMSA officials, traditionally, gathering pipelines range in diameter from about 2 to 12 inches and operate at pressures that range from about 5 to 800 pounds per square inch (psi). These pipelines tend to be located in rural areas but can also be located in urban areas. PHMSA estimates there are 200,000 miles of gas gathering pipelines and 30,000 to 40,000 miles of hazardous liquid gathering pipelines.

- *Transmission pipelines.* Transmission pipelines carry hazardous liquid or natural gas, sometimes over hundreds of miles, to communities and large-volume users (e.g., factories).[3] For natural gas transmission pipelines, compression stations located periodically along the pipeline maintain product pressure. Similarly, pumping stations along hazardous liquid transmission pipelines maintain product flow. Transmission pipelines tend to have the largest diameters and pressures of any type of pipeline, generally ranging from 12 inches to 42 inches in diameter and operating at pressures ranging from 400 to 1440 psi.[4] PHMSA has estimated there are more than 400,000 miles of gas and hazardous liquid transmission pipelines.

- *Distribution pipelines.* Gas distribution pipelines continue to transport natural gas to residential, commercial, and industrial customers, splitting off from transmission pipelines. These pipelines tend to be smaller, sometimes less than 1 inch in diameter, and operate at lower pressures—0.25 to 100 psi.[5] PHMSA has estimated there are roughly 2 million miles of distribution pipelines, most of which are intrastate pipelines. There are no hazardous liquid distribution pipelines.

---

[3]For the purposes of this report, we use the term transmission pipeline to refer to both hazardous liquid and natural gas pipelines carrying product over long distances to users.

[4]However, there are transmission pipelines smaller than 12 inches in diameter and other pipelines that operate at pressures greater than 1440 psi. In addition, we have reported on safety regulations for certain transmission pipelines that operate at lower stress. For more information, see GAO, *Safety Effects of Less Prescriptive Requirements for Low-Stress Natural Gas Transmission Pipelines Are Uncertain*, GAO-12-389R (Washington, D.C.: Feb. 16, 2012).

[5]However, some distribution pipelines can be as large as 24 inches in diameter and operate at higher pressures (i.e., over 350 psi).

Figure 1: Pipeline System

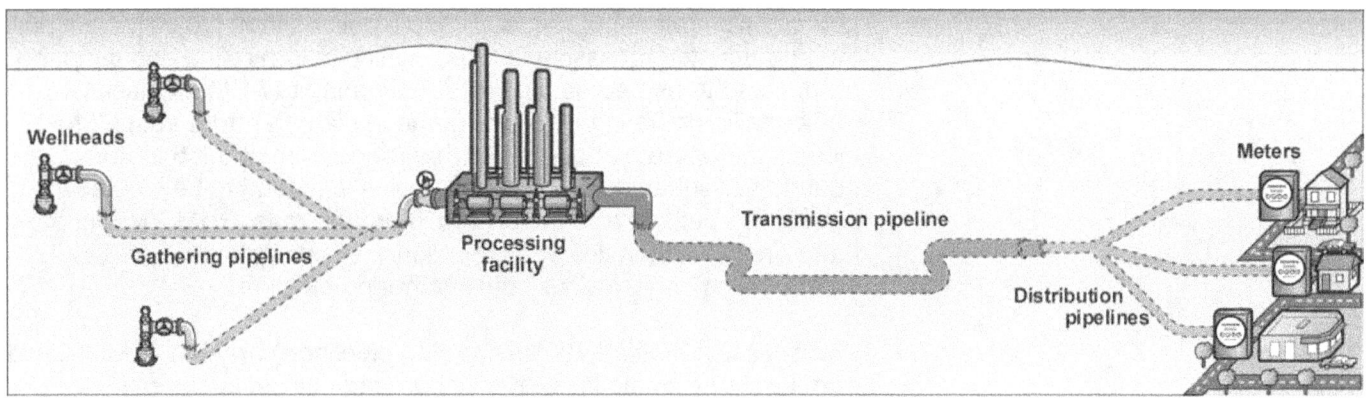

Source: PHMSA

In recent years, shale oil and gas exploration and related development has led to the construction of new infrastructure, including gathering pipelines. Shale oil and gas refers to product that is trapped within underground shale formations; these fine-grain sedimentary rocks can be rich sources of oil and natural gas. Over the past decade, improvements in drilling technologies have allowed access to large volumes of shale oil and gas deposits in several states that were previously uneconomical to access.

In terms of fatalities and injuries, pipelines are the safest mode for transporting hazardous liquids and natural gas. From 2004 to 2010, there was an average of about 16 fatalities per year for all incidents reported to PHMSA.[6] In comparison, in 2009, over 3,000 fatalities resulted from incidents involving large trucks carrying freight and about 700 additional fatalities resulted from freight railroad incidents. Yet, pipelines face a number of risks—such as corrosion and excavation damage—that can damage the pipeline's integrity and result in leaks and ruptures. A leak generally occurs with a slow release of product over a small area. A rupture involves the sometimes sudden development of a breach in the pipeline, which may cause hazardous liquids to spill or gas to spark and

---

[6]In its regulations, PHMSA refers to the release of natural gas from a pipeline as an "incident" and a spill from a hazardous liquid pipeline as an "accident." (49 CFR Part 195, Subpart B). For simplicity, this report will refer to both as "incidents." PHMSA tracks summary level statistics for pipeline incidents that meet certain reporting criteria, such as those incidents resulting in a fatality.

ignite, resulting in an explosion.[7] Such an incident occurred in San Bruno, California, on September 9, 2010, damaging or destroying over 100 homes and killing 8 people.

PHMSA administers the national regulatory program to ensure the safe transportation of hazardous liquid and gas by pipeline. PHMSA carries out its mission through regulation,[8] national consensus standards, research, education, inspections, and enforcement when safety problems or regulatory violations are found. The agency employs over 200 staff in its pipeline safety program, about half of whom inspect hazardous liquid and gas pipelines for compliance with safety regulations. Besides PHMSA, over 300 state inspectors also help oversee pipelines and ensure safety.

In general, PHMSA performs its oversight role using uniform, minimum safety standards that all pipeline operators regulated by PHMSA must meet, as well as a supplemental risk-based regulatory program termed "integrity management" for pipelines in "high-consequence areas" where an incident would have greater consequences for public safety or the environment. The uniform, minimum safety standards include specifications for the design, construction, testing, inspection, operation, and maintenance of pipelines. For example, operators are required to install and maintain pipeline markers to clearly show a pipeline's right-of-way. In addition, the risk-based integrity management programs for hazardous liquid and natural gas transmission pipelines and natural gas distribution pipelines require operators to systematically identify and mitigate risks to pipeline segments located in high-consequence areas, which are defined differently for three types of pipelines.

- High-consequence areas for hazardous liquid pipelines include areas of highly populated areas, other populated areas, navigable waterways, and areas unusually sensitive to environmental damage.

- High-consequence areas for natural gas transmission pipelines include highly populated or frequently used areas, such as parks.

---

[7]The risks and consequences posed by gas and hazardous liquids incidents also differ. Gas tends to ignite more easily, resulting in more explosions. Hazardous liquids ignite less easily, but can spill onto and pollute the environment.

[8]Part 191 (Gas Reporting), Part 192 (Gas), Part 193 (Liquid Natural Gas), Part 194 (Liquid Facility Response Plans), and Part 195 (Hazardous Liquid) of Title 49 of the Code of Federal Regulations.

- Most natural gas distribution pipelines would generally be considered to be in high-consequence areas, as defined under the transmission pipelines regulations, since they are typically located in highly populated areas.

PHMSA regulates hazardous liquid and natural gas gathering pipelines—using uniform, minimum standards—based on their proximity to populated and environmentally sensitive areas. For natural gas gathering pipelines,[9] PHMSA uses class locations—the same classification system used for natural gas transmission and distribution pipelines. (See table 1.) Under this system, PHMSA generally regulates onshore natural gas gathering pipelines in Class 2, 3, or 4 locations. For hazardous liquid gathering pipelines, PHMSA regulates those pipelines in incorporated and unincorporated cities, towns, and villages; pipeline segments that cross a waterway currently used for commercial navigation; and certain rural gathering pipelines within one-quarter mile of environmentally sensitive areas. This includes high-consequence areas, as defined for the hazardous liquid integrity management program. High-consequence areas can also be in Class 1, 2, 3, or 4 locations, which can entail different reporting requirements. For example, gathering pipeline operators in high-consequence areas that are in Class 1 locations are not required to report data on pipeline-related incidents, including fatality, injury, and property damage information.

Table 1: PHMSA Class Designations for Gas Pipelines

Class designation	Location features
Class 1	An offshore area or any location with 10 or fewer buildings intended for human occupancy within 220 yards of the centerline of the pipeline.
Class 2	Any location with more than 10 but fewer than 46 buildings intended for human occupancy within 220 yards of the centerline of the pipeline.
Class 3	Any location with more than 46 buildings intended for human occupancy within 220 yards of a pipeline, or an area where the pipeline lies within 100 yards of either a building or a small, well-defined outside area (such as a playground) that is occupied by 20 or more persons at least 5 days a week for 10 weeks in any 12-month period.
Class 4	Any location where unit buildings with four or more stories above ground are prevalent.

Source: 49 C.F.R. § 192 5.

---

[9]49 C.F.R. §192.5.

Under the current regulatory system, PHMSA does not regulate most gathering pipelines in the United States based on their location. For example, out of the more than 200,000 estimated miles of natural gas gathering pipelines, PHMSA regulates roughly 20,000 miles. Similarly, of the 30,000 to 40,000 estimated miles of hazardous liquid gathering pipelines, PHMSA regulates about 4,000 miles.[10] However, according to PHMSA officials, the agency has the authority to collect data on all onshore hazardous liquid and gas gathering pipelines,[11] even though it generally does not regulate gas gathering pipelines in Class 1 locations or hazardous liquid gathering pipelines not located in high-consequence areas.

Generally, PHMSA retains full responsibility for inspecting and enforcing regulations on interstate pipelines. However, states may be authorized to conduct inspections for interstate pipelines, as well as inspections and associated enforcement for intrastate pipelines. States can also promulgate regulations for intrastate pipelines, including gathering pipelines. PHMSA has arrangements with 48 states, the District of Columbia, and Puerto Rico to assist with overseeing interstate, intrastate, or both interstate and intrastate pipelines. These arrangements, in which states act as "agents" for PHMSA, can cover hazardous liquid pipelines only, gas pipelines only, or both (see fig. 2). State pipeline safety offices are allowed to issue regulations supplementing or extending federal regulations, but these state regulations must be at least as stringent as the minimum federal regulations. If a state wants to issue regulations that apply to pipelines that PHMSA does not regulate, such as unregulated gathering pipelines, it must do so under its own (state) authority.

---

[10]According to PHMSA officials, Alaska, California, Louisiana, and Oklahoma have the majority of federally unregulated gathering pipeline mileage in the United States.

[11]49 U.S.C. §60102(b).This report refers to gathering pipelines that are not regulated by PHMSA but that PHMSA is not prohibited by law from regulating. Nonregulated gathering pipelines are typically unregulated Class 1 pipelines found in rural locations where there are no or low populations.

Figure 2: Interstate and Intrastate Agents for PHMSA

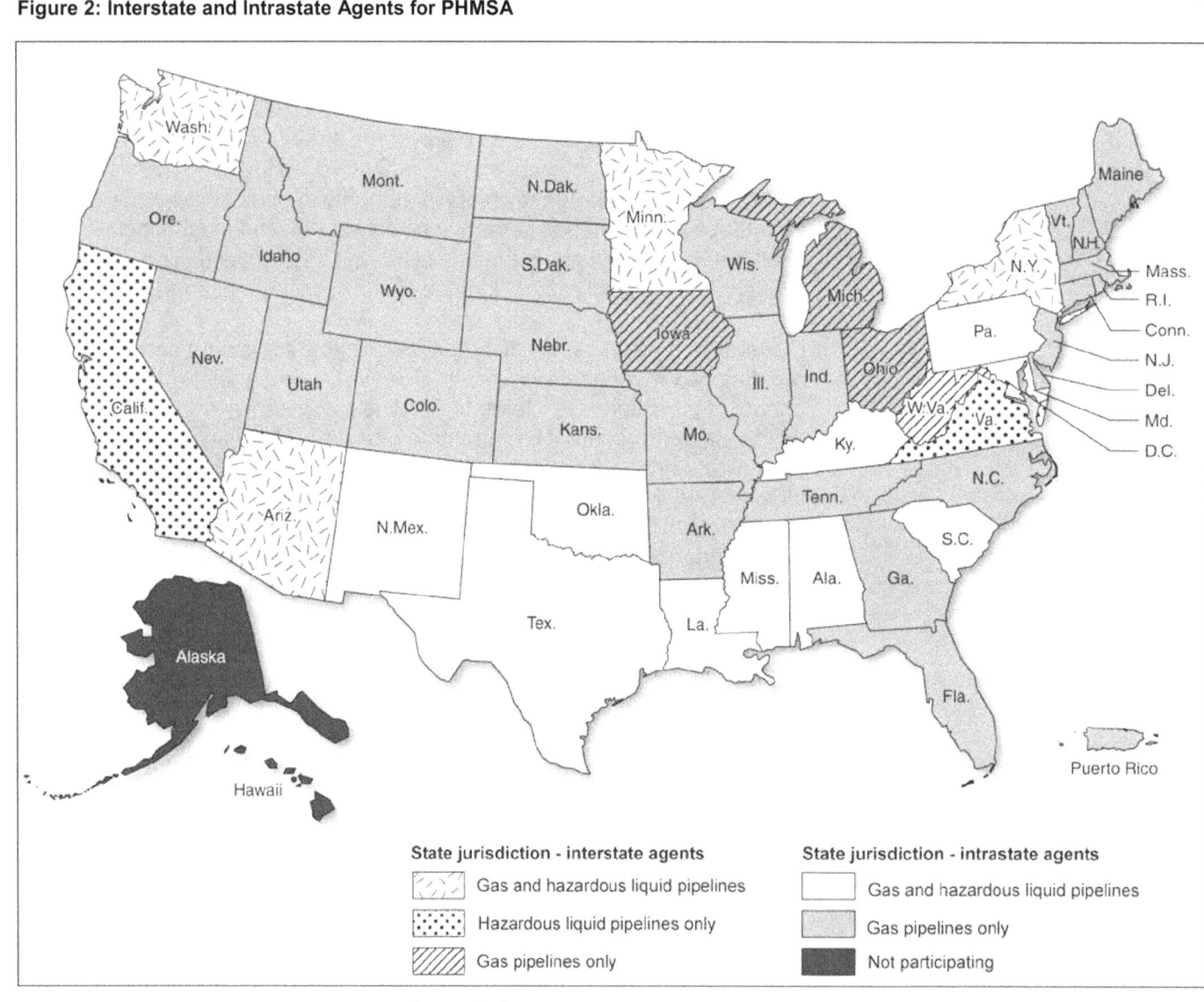

State jurisdiction - interstate agents
- Gas and hazardous liquid pipelines
- Hazardous liquid pipelines only
- Gas pipelines only

State jurisdiction - intrastate agents
- Gas and hazardous liquid pipelines
- Gas pipelines only
- Not participating

Sources: U.S. DOT (information) and Map Resources (map).

Limited Information on Safety Risks and Changing Operational Environments Are Leading PHMSA to Consider Collecting Data

Limited Information

While gathering pipelines generally pose lower safety risks than other types of pipelines, PHMSA does not collect comprehensive data on safety risks associated with gathering pipelines. In response to GAO's survey, state pipeline safety agencies cited construction quality, maintenance practices, unknown or uncertain locations, and limited or no information on current pipeline integrity as safety risks for federally unregulated gathering pipelines.[12] Operators of unregulated gathering pipelines are not required by federal law to report information on such risk factors. Consequently, federal and state pipeline safety officials do not know the extent to which individual operators collect such information and use it to monitor the safety of their pipelines. In our survey of 52 state agencies, 39 agencies—10 monitoring hazardous liquid and 29 monitoring natural gas—responded that they had onshore gathering pipelines that PHMSA does not regulate located in their state. (See app. II for a summary of our survey results.) For these 39 agencies, four of the five top responses cited the following risk factors for onshore unregulated gathering pipelines as among the highest public safety risks.

- *Construction quality.* Eighteen state agencies reported that the quality of installation procedures and construction materials is a moderate or high safety risk for unregulated gathering pipelines. The construction phase of pipeline installation is critical to ensure the long-term integrity of the pipeline because the installation methods and materials used in pipeline construction affect the pipeline's resistance to deterioration over time. For example, one inspection requirement for regulated

---

[12]Risk is defined by PHMSA as the combination of the likelihood and the consequence of a specified hazard being realized.

pipelines is that they may not be installed unless they have been visually inspected at the site of installation to ensure that they are not damaged in a manner that could impair their strength or reduce their serviceability.[13] This requirement does not currently apply to unregulated gathering pipelines.

- *Maintenance practices.* Sixteen state agencies reported that the extent to which pipeline operators maintain their pipelines is a moderate or high safety risk for unregulated gathering pipelines. According to agency officials, after a pipeline is installed and operational, periodic maintenance—such as inspecting and testing equipment—is important to prevent leaks and ruptures and could extend the operating life of a pipeline. Furthermore, preventive measures and repairs conducted on unregulated gathering pipelines, as well as a record of such activities, could provide useful information on the safety and history of a given gathering pipeline.

- *Location.* Sixteen state agencies reported that the unknown or uncertain location of unregulated gathering pipelines presents a moderate or high safety risk. Although individual operators may know the locations of unregulated pipelines, state and local safety agencies may not know or may be uncertain about the locations and mileage of unregulated pipeline infrastructure in their communities. This information is particularly useful for "Call Before You Dig" programs operated by states and localities. If unregulated gathering pipelines are unmarked and program officials do not know the location of the pipelines, businesses and citizens may damage a pipeline during excavation, which could result in an incident—including fatalities, injuries, or damage to property or the environment—as well as the shutting down of the pipeline for repair.

- *Pipeline integrity.* Sixteen state agencies reported that not knowing or having limited knowledge about the integrity—the current condition—of unregulated gathering pipelines is a moderate or high safety risk. Factors that affect the integrity of all pipelines—such as excavation damage and corrosion—also affect gathering pipelines. For example, excavation damage to a pipeline from nearby digging activities (see fig. 3) is the leading cause of pipeline incidents and, as previously noted, the uncertain location of unregulated gathering pipelines may

---

[13]49 C.F.R. §195.206 (Hazardous Liquid) and 49 C.F.R. §192.307 (Gas).

increase the potential for such damage. Furthermore, corrosion can occur on the inside and outside of metal pipelines and is not easily identified without appropriate pipeline assessments. From 2004 through 2010, corrosion was reported as the cause of about 60 percent—or nine incidents—of regulated gas gathering pipeline incidents. Generally, pipeline experts we spoke with said limited information on the integrity of unregulated gathering pipelines prevents analysis to assess the internal and external condition of these pipelines.

Figure 3: Excavation Damage

Source: Colorado Public Utilities Commission.

Changing Operational Environments

According to responses to our survey and interviews with industry officials and representatives, land-use changes and the increased extraction of oil and natural gas from shale deposits are two changes in the operating environments that could increase the safety risks for unregulated gathering pipelines.

- *Land-use changes.* The fifth top response reported by state pipeline safety agencies we surveyed was that increased urbanization has caused rural areas to become more densely populated and, in some cases, developments have encroached on existing pipeline rights-of-way. (See fig. 4.) Nineteen state agencies reported land-use changes as a moderate or high risk for federally unregulated gathering pipelines. Federal and state pipeline safety officials we spoke with are concerned about the safety and proximity of people who work and live near pipeline rights-of-way. For example, one state official stated that although a new housing or business development can change a location's designation from Class 1 to a higher class that would then fall under PHMSA's jurisdiction, the operator may not be aware of the development and therefore would not monitor and apply more stringent regulations along that pipeline.

Figure 4: Changing Land Use around Pipelines

1990

2002

Sources: U.S. Geological Survey (left) and National Geospatial-Intelligence Agency (right)

- *Increased extraction of oil and gas from shale deposits.* According to pipeline industry officials and representatives we interviewed, the increased extraction of oil and natural gas from shale deposits poses an increased risk to the public, partly because of the development of new and larger gathering pipeline infrastructure. Deposits of oil and natural gas have become increasingly important energy sources in the United States over the past decade (see fig. 5). According to the U.S. Energy Information Administration, shale gas accounted for 16 percent of the total domestic natural gas supply in 2009 and is projected to increase to approximately 47 percent by 2035. This extraction has led to drilling and production in regions of the country that have previously seen little or no such activity. As a result of this ongoing activity, as well as future growth projections, state and federal safety officials we interviewed identified new gathering pipelines related to shale development as a potential public safety risk. The risk

GAO-12-388 Pipeline Safety

is primarily due to the characteristics and quantity of pipeline infrastructure required to support this new production. Specifically, some of these new gathering pipelines have larger diameters and operate at higher pressures that are equivalent to traditional transmission pipelines, but without the regulatory requirements.[14] For instance, an October 2010 report[15] on pipeline issues and concerns in Fort Worth stated that some gathering pipelines were as large as 24 inches in diameter with maximum allowable operating pressures similar to those for transmission pipelines. Those gathering pipelines were currently exempt from federal integrity management rules, which require some form of pipeline integrity assessment at least once every 7 years, and clearly define how and when problems found during these assessments are to be reported and repaired.

---

[14]49 C.F.R. § 195.452 (Hazardous Materials) & 49 C.F.R. Part 192 Subpart O (Gas).

[15]Accufacts Inc. and Pipeline Safety Trust, *The State of Natural Gas Pipelines in Fort Worth*, a special report prepared at the request of the Fort Worth League of Neighborhoods, Fort Worth, October 2010.

Figure 5: Current and Prospective Shale Gas Regions

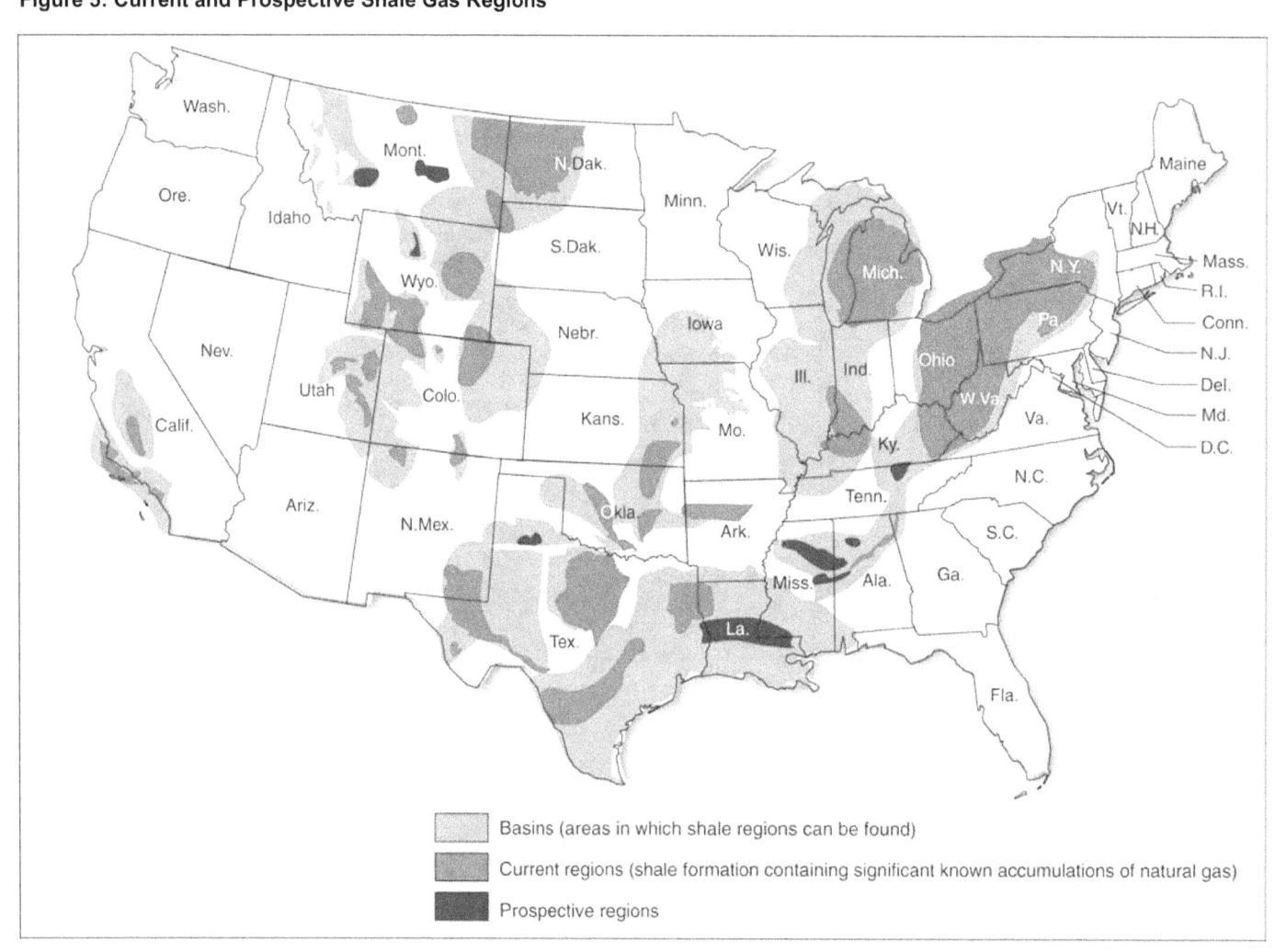

Basins (areas in which shale regions can be found)

Current regions (shale formation containing significant known accumulations of natural gas)

Prospective regions

Sources: Energy Information Administration (information) and Map Resources (map)

Note: This map depicts shale gas regions, where shale gas is known or thought to exist, but does not indicate where extraction is actually occurring.

PHMSA Is Considering Collecting Data

PHMSA officials stated that they are considering collecting data on federally unregulated onshore gathering pipelines to better understand and evaluate the safety risks posed by these pipelines. Although PHMSA has the legal authority to collect data on unregulated gathering pipelines, the agency is not required and has not yet exercised its authority to do so. PHMSA officials reported that, instead of collecting such data, the agency was focusing on the development of integrity management requirements

GAO-12-388 Pipeline Safety

and improved data collection for higher-risk transmission and distribution pipelines. However, PHMSA officials reported that there is value in having data for unregulated pipelines similar to what is currently collected on regulated pipelines, such as pipeline characteristics and reportable information on incidents—including the location, cause, and consequences of these incidents.

In addition, PHMSA issued Advanced Notices of Proposed Rulemakings (ANPRM) for onshore hazardous liquid and gas pipelines in October 2010 and August 2011, respectively.[16] For these proposed rulemakings, PHMSA has sought comment on, among other things, whether to extend regulation or other requirements to currently federally unregulated gathering pipelines. Concerning potential data collection, the ANPRMs sought comment on whether to require the submission of annual, incident, and safety-related condition reports on federally unregulated gathering pipelines, as well as on whether to establish a new, risk-based regime of safety requirements for large-diameter, high-pressure gas gathering pipelines, including those pipelines in rural locations.[17] While the ANPRMs did not seek comment on exactly what new data to collect, PHMSA officials reported that the information would likely be similar to what is currently collected on regulated gathering pipelines and that they plan to issue final rules in late 2012. In the event that reporting requirements are adopted, PHMSA officials stated that gathering pipeline data would likely be collected on a state-by-state basis, which could later be expanded to the national level. However, PHMSA's plans for collecting data are preliminary, and the extent to which PHMSA will collect data sufficient to evaluate the potential safety risks associated with these pipelines is uncertain.

Currently, PHMSA collects annual, incident, and safety-related condition data on regulated pipelines. The specific types of safety-related data collected for regulated pipelines include the operator, pipeline system description, mileage by class location, diameter size, operating pressure, incident location, number of injuries and fatalities, property damage, and

---

[16]75 *Fed. Reg.* 63774 (Oct. 18, 2010) and 76 *Fed. Reg.* 53086 (Aug. 25, 2011).

[17]PHMSA granted extensions to the comment period for both of these ANPRMs (see 76 *Fed. Reg.* 303 (Jan. 4, 2011) and 76 *Fed. Reg.* 70953 (Nov. 16, 2011)). The ANPRM related to hazardous liquids closed for comment in February 2011 and the ANPRM for gas in January 2012.

assessments conducted. These data help federal and state safety officials and pipeline operators increase the safety of these pipelines by better identifying and quantifying safety risks, as well as by implementing mitigation strategies, and addressing potential regulatory needs. It is for these same reasons that PHMSA, state, and some industry officials reported that collecting similar data for unregulated gathering pipelines would be beneficial. PHMSA officials also reported that in the event the agency started collecting data on unregulated onshore gathering pipelines, their current data reporting system could accommodate such a collection and not require large changes for regulators or operators. On the other hand, a few operators and industry groups we met with expressed concerns over the burden that new data reporting would represent. Before any potential data collection reporting requirements could be enacted, PHMSA and the Office of Management and Budget would review and evaluate the value of such information and associated burdens on industry. PHMSA officials said that while many operators should already have information on their gathering pipelines readily available, it would still be important to communicate with operators and take steps to minimize burdens in collecting new gathering pipeline data.

Some benefits of collecting such pipeline data can be seen through additional analysis of currently collected data. For example, PHMSA's data on regulated pipelines indicate that more onshore reportable incidents, as well as total property damage, occur on transmission and distribution pipelines, than on regulated gathering pipelines (see figs. 6 and 7). Although the number of reportable incidents for regulated gas gathering pipelines is lower than for other regulated pipelines, the value of total property damage increased in the past few years. In 2010, these reportable incidents accounted for, on average, about $1.8 million in property damage per incident.

Figure 6: Number of Incidents for All Federally Regulated Pipeline Systems, 2004 through 2010

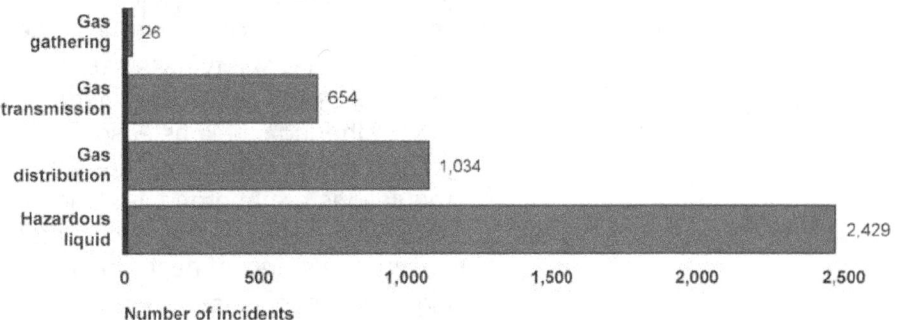

Number of incidents

Source: GAO analysis of PHMSA data.

Note: Regulated hazardous liquid data is not collected, segregated, and reported to PHMSA by type of pipeline (i.e., gathering and transmission). Also, there are no hazardous liquid distribution pipeline systems. Therefore, incident data for regulated hazardous liquid transmission and gathering pipelines is combined.

Figure 7: Total Property Damage for All Regulated Pipeline Systems, 2004 through 2010

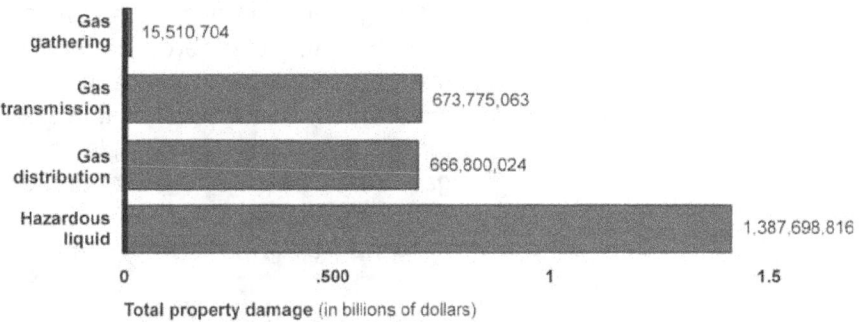

Total property damage (in billions of dollars)

Source: GAO analysis of PHMSA data.

Note: Regulated hazardous liquid data is not collected, segregated, and reported to PHMSA by type of pipeline (i.e., gathering and transmission). Also, there are no hazardous liquid distribution pipeline systems. Therefore, property damage data for regulated hazardous liquid transmission and gathering pipelines is combined.

Another benefit of collecting annual, incident, and safety-related condition pipeline data is an increased ability to assess and manage risks. We have previously reported on the importance of assessing and managing risks, including quantifying those risks using data.[18] Data are instrumental in quantifying risks and can reduce uncertainty in assumptions and policy judgments (e.g., safety threats and the likelihood that they will be realized).[19] PHMSA officials reported that collecting data could help to determine the safety risks associated with federally unregulated gathering pipelines, such as tracking injuries, fatalities, and property damage for new gathering pipelines associated with shale development, and whether current safety regulations are appropriate. Related to whether current regulations are appropriate, Congress recently mandated that DOT review the sufficiency of existing federal and state laws and regulations to ensure the safety of hazardous liquid and gas gathering pipelines.[20] Two industry associations reported that such data collection could help better ensure that federal pipeline programs are appropriately targeted at mitigating safety risks, cost-effective, and not unnecessarily broad in scope. Quantitatively assessing risks could also allow for a ranking and prioritizing of safety risks facing gathering pipelines in a manner that is currently not possible.

Besides PHMSA, states may collect data on unregulated gathering pipelines, but the scope and nature of this data collection can vary. Although the federal government is responsible for setting minimum pipeline safety standards, states can adopt additional or stricter safety standards for intrastate pipeline facilities and transportation—including standards for data collection. For example, Texas's state regulation further defined that the state's safety jurisdiction for onshore gas gathering pipelines begins after the first point of measurement—where the product is first measured to determine the volume being extracted from the well—and is based on population, which is stricter than the

---

[18]GAO, *Risk Management: Strengthening the Use of Risk Management Principles in Homeland* Security, GAO-08-904T (Washington, D.C.: June 25, 2008).

[19]GAO, *Homeland Security: DHS Risk-Based Grant Methodology Is Reasonable, But Current Version's Measure of Vulnerability is Limited*, GAO-08-852 (Washington, D.C.: June 27, 2008)

[20]Pipeline Safety, Regulatory Certainty, and Job Creation Act of 2011, Pub. L. No. 112-90, §21, 125 Stat. 1904, 1917 (2011).

federal standard.[21] Our survey revealed that only 3 of the 39 state agencies reported that they collect and analyze comprehensive pipeline spill and release data on federally unregulated pipelines. Such information can be used to help reduce future incidents. Additionally, the National Association of Pipeline Safety Representatives (NAPSR) recently conducted a nationwide survey[22] to determine which state requirements match or exceed federal pipeline safety requirements. The survey reported that neither states nor the District of Columbia collected comprehensive data on federally unregulated gathering pipelines, as is required for federally regulated pipelines.

States Could Benefit from Sharing Safety Practices

State pipeline safety agencies reported using five safety practices most frequently to help ensure the safety of onshore hazardous liquid and gas gathering pipelines not regulated by PHMSA, according to our survey of state agencies[23] (see fig. 8). Several of these practices are designed to counter previously discussed safety risks; for example, implementing damage prevention programs can lower the risks of excavation damage.[24] Although these practices were cited most frequently, one-third or less of the state pipeline safety agencies with unregulated gathering pipelines use any one of these practices. For instance, 13 of the 39 state pipeline safety agencies with unregulated gathering pipelines in their state reported using the most frequently cited safety practice—damage

---

[21]Texas Administrative Code, Title 16, Part 1, Chapter 8 Subchapter A, Rule Section 8.5. Although the federal government is responsible for setting minimum pipeline safety standards, Texas, and other certified states, can adopt additional or more stringent safety standards for intrastate pipeline facilities and intrastate pipeline transportation. (49 U.S.C. §60104(c)). However, any intrastate safety standards adopted by Texas and other certified states must be compatible with the federal standards.

[22]National Association of Pipeline Safety Representatives and the National Association of Regulatory Utility Commissioners, *Compendium of State Pipeline Safety Requirements & Initiatives Providing Increased Public Safety Levels compared to Code of Federal Regulations*, 1st Edition 2011 (Sept. 30, 2011).

[23]These practices refer to state pipeline safety practices that are more stringent than PHMSA's regulatory requirements and to central activities, programs, or other policies that can help ensure the safety of various onshore pipelines. We recognize that in some states a practice may be part of the state's regulations, while in other states, such practices are separate from regulations.

[24]When we discuss safety practices, we refer to those safety practices that state agencies described as being relevant for helping ensure the safety of gathering pipelines. Some of these same practices may also be applied to other types of pipelines.

prevention programs. Additionally, some of the state agencies that reported using safety practices also responded that, overall, they had promulgated safety requirements for onshore gathering pipelines that were more stringent than those provided by PHMSA.

Figure 8: Most Frequently Used Safety Practices by States for Gathering Pipelines

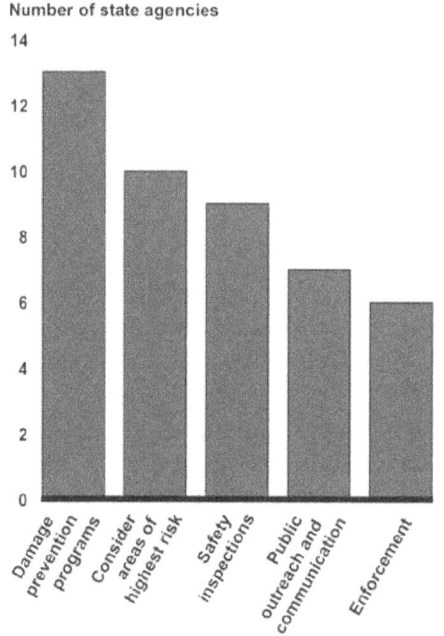

Number of state agencies

Most frequently used safety practices

Source: GAO.

- *Damage prevention programs.* Thirteen state agencies[25] reported that they implement and enforce a damage prevention program as a practice to help ensure pipeline safety. Damage prevention programs can help mitigate risks and increase safety through a number of activities. For example, damage prevention programs can help reduce the risk of excavation damage by encouraging citizens and other parties to collect information to help identify pipeline locations before digging begins. Damage prevention programs can also include

---

[25]When discussing the number of state agencies that reported using a given safety practice, these 13 agencies are a subset of the 39 state agencies that reported having unregulated gathering pipelines.

GAO-12-388 Pipeline Safety

marking the rights-of-way for pipelines—including gathering pipelines—above ground to further reduce the likelihood of excavation damage (see fig. 9). States have developed or participated in damage prevention programs to help reduce instances of excavation damage, including damage to gathering pipelines. For example, Colorado has participated in the national One-Call program to reduce excavation damage. One-Call programs enable citizens and organizations to call an 811 number to notify utilities, pipeline operators, and others about the location and nature of planned digging. Utility, pipeline, or other organization members can then mark where underground pipelines run before any digging begins. Colorado pipeline safety officials reported that some calls related to the marking of regulated and unregulated gathering pipelines. As to the effectiveness of One-Call programs, the Common Ground Alliance has reported that, in 2010, when an excavator notified a call center before digging, damage occurred less than 1 percent of the time.[26]

---

[26]Common Ground Alliance, *DIRT Annual Report for 2010* (Alexandria, VA, 2011). The Common Ground Alliance is an association dedicated to ensuring public safety, environmental protection, and the integrity of services by promoting effective damage prevention practices.

Figure 9: Pipeline Marker

Source: GAO

- *Considering areas of highest risk.* Ten state agencies reported they consider the areas of highest risk to effectively target resources as a safety practice. This approach can help address risks, such as corrosion and a lack of periodic maintenance, by directing oversight to those pipelines that could have the most serious consequences in the event of an incident.[27] In addition, considering the areas of highest risk could help address potential safety risks from new gathering pipeline infrastructure associated with shale development. For example, considering risk factors associated with larger pipelines, operating pressures, and location could help determine the actual risks posed by these new pipelines. Indeed, some of PHMSA's more recent pipeline safety regulations addressing integrity management and high-consequence areas account for risk factors to help

---

[27]While data are helpful for assessing risks, PHMSA and state agency officials mentioned using other information sources to qualitatively assess risks, such as guidance and protocols and general pipeline traits like location.

determine which regulations might apply to a particular pipeline.[28] Industry officials reported that it is more effective to target higher-risk areas than to allocate resources across all areas. Officials with the Texas Oil and Gas Association added that the risk of a pipeline incident in a heavily populated area warrants more attention than the risk of a similar incident in a sparsely populated area. This practice also acknowledges that gathering pipelines run through a wide variety of environments with varying risk levels (see fig. 10). Some states are overseeing pipelines based on identified safety risks. For example, safety compliance and enforcement staff at the Texas Railroad Commission[29] reported that inspecting pipeline systems based on identified risks allows the state to inspect some pipelines less frequently, such as pipelines made from newer and safer materials, have advanced monitoring technology, or are located away from populations—like some rural gathering pipelines. Using these risk-based safety evaluations also enables Texas Railroad Commission inspectors to concentrate on higher-risk pipeline systems.

---

[28]PHMSA's integrity management program for transmission pipelines already requires operators to systematically manage risks to their pipelines in areas where an accident could have the highest consequences. In our past work on pipeline safety, we have supported the use of risk-based methodologies for PHMSA's regulation of the pipeline industry. See GAO, *Natural Gas Pipeline Safety: Risk-Based Standards Should Allow Operators to Better Tailor Reassessments to Pipeline Threats*, GAO-06-945 (Washington, D.C.: Sept. 8, 2006).

[29]Formed in 1891, the Texas Railroad Commission regulates the safety of intrastate natural gas pipelines and hazardous liquids pipelines in Texas. Commission staff conduct safety inspections of pipeline operators, issue compliance guidance, and enforce rules for Texas's pipeline excavation damage prevention program.

Figure 10: Examples of Rural and Residential Gathering Pipeline Operational Environments near Dallas-Fort Worth

Source: GAO.

- *Safety inspections.* Nine state agencies reported they conduct recurring, scheduled, or unscheduled safety inspections of hazardous liquid and gas operators as another safety practice. NAPSR officials reported that safety inspections can be regularly scheduled inspections, during which inspectors check system components, specialized inspections (i.e., integrity management) aimed at higher-risk areas, or random checks. These inspections can also help

GAO-12-388 Pipeline Safety

address risks related to the installation and construction quality of a pipeline by ensuring that the pipeline is structurally sound and shows no evidence of questionable materials or other problems, such as corrosion and excavation damage. PHMSA has recommended that state pipeline safety agencies perform periodic surprise inspections on new pipeline construction to determine whether operators are complying with construction requirements. Inspectors with the Texas Railroad Commission, in addition to sampling on-site pipeline facilities in the field, also review pipeline operators' records and documentation on selected pipeline systems for compliance with federal and state pipeline safety regulations. These risk-based safety evaluations have included the construction of gathering pipelines related to shale development and pipelines not regulated by PHMSA. Such evaluations also help ensure that operators maintain an up-to-date and consistent document records system for installation, operations, and emergency response (see fig. 11).

Figure 11: Gathering Pipeline Construction Documentation in Texas

Source: GAO.

- *Public outreach and communication.* Seven state agencies reported they engage in outreach or other communication with communities and citizens to boost awareness and knowledge of pipeline safety practices they use. The Common Ground Alliance has reported on the importance of outreach, including the use of structured education programs, targeted mailings, and paid advertising. These and other outreach methods can also underscore the importance of other safety practices, such as damage prevention and One-Call programs. These outreach efforts can involve a number of methods and include educating and engaging the public. In Colorado, Damage Prevention Councils have hosted monthly meetings and participated in local community events—such as educational seminars, parades, and trade shows—to help educate citizens on pipeline safety. Another Colorado entity active in damage prevention is the Colorado Pipeline Association, which comprises pipeline operators dedicated to promoting pipeline safety by providing information for excavators, state residents, businesses, emergency responders, and public officials. In one community, according to a PHMSA official, citizens viewed state safety officials as an objective and neutral party that provided information and perspectives on the planned construction of gathering pipelines. In tandem with private operators, the state officials were able to answer citizen questions and address concerns.

- *Enforcement.* Six state agencies reported a safety practice of establishing a system of escalated enforcement to enhance and increase regulatory attention on operators that have experienced incidents. A pipeline expert we interviewed said that promoting an effective enforcement program was necessary to help ensure pipeline safety. A system of escalated enforcement can enhance and increase regulatory attention on pipeline operators with safety violations. One state pipeline safety official reported that making such attention public can bring additional pressure on and provide incentives for a company to maintain and operate its infrastructure safely. One PHMSA official reported that although many states do not have an enforcement program as elaborate as PHMSA, states with stronger enforcement programs have more of an impact on the operators to increase safety. Pipeline operators may have procedures and established contacts with local enforcement personnel in order to act appropriately to halt dangerous excavation activities that may damage pipelines and potentially cause an immediate threat to life or property. Regarding federally unregulated gathering pipelines, one Colorado official reported that because gathering pipeline companies operate pipelines and conduct excavation work, they would be subject to any necessary enforcement due to safety violations.

However, sharing of information among states on the safety practices they use for unregulated gathering pipelines appears to be limited. Some state and PHMSA officials we interviewed had limited awareness of what other states were doing to help ensure the safety of gathering pipelines not regulated by PHMSA. For example, pipeline safety officials we interviewed had limited awareness of other state programs—sometimes even for an adjacent state—even if those programs were intended to address common risks, such as reducing excavation damage and corrosion. PHMSA officials were likewise unable to report on the safety practices that many states use or on states' regulations that were more stringent than federal requirements. PHMSA's website holds a wealth of information on various pipeline safety topics, including recent pipeline forums and industry research, incident investigations, and other information. However, information targeted at gathering pipelines, including relevant safety practices and state activities, is limited.[30] In addition, all related information could be grouped to decrease time spent searching and scanning. Currently, there is no central PHMSA web page or resource for gathering pipelines, regulated or unregulated—possibly due, in part, to the lower safety risks that regulated gathering pipelines have posed to people and property when compared with other pipelines, like transmission pipelines. PHMSA officials said that its website also focuses on pipelines that PHMSA regulates but excludes most gathering pipelines. PHMSA has considered the development of a website to help facilitate sharing information among states. While this project is still in the planning stages and not targeted at gathering pipelines, it could be a resource to share program and safety practices among states and PHMSA.

Increased communication and information sharing about pipeline safety practices could boost the use of those practices in states with unregulated gathering pipelines. As previously discussed, even the safety practice that our survey respondents reported using most frequently—implementing a damage prevention program—was used by just 13 of the 39 responding state pipeline safety agencies with unregulated gathering pipelines in their

---

[30]Websites that are limited tend to be less usable. Usable websites—that is, those that are planned and designed to collect data on what users need and include various user-centered design methods, among other things—ensure that needed information is available and clearly displayed. These standards are based on guidance posted on the U.S. Department of Health and Human Services' websites, http://www.usability.gov, a source for information on usability and user-centered design. It provides guidance and tools on how to make websites and other communication systems more usable and useful.

state. The other four safety practices cited are reportedly used even less. Improved information sharing among states and PHMSA could help spread information on how these safety practices—which are also used for regulated pipelines—could be applied to unregulated gathering pipelines, thereby benefiting other states with unregulated gathering pipelines. We have previously reported on the value of organizations reporting and sharing safety information as part of encouraging a wider safety culture.[31] Safety culture can include organizational awareness of safety and open communication. The benefits of a strong safety culture have widespread applicability, including in other transportation areas—such as aviation and transit. PHMSA could serve to facilitate feedback and evaluate safety information related to unregulated gathering pipelines in states. By collecting information on safety practices and other information relevant to unregulated gathering pipelines, PHMSA could increase the potential for identifying systemic issues, disseminating lessons learned, and improving pipeline safety across the country. PHMSA officials reported that, in the past, similar online and educational efforts in other areas have resulted in increasing education and information sharing among state pipeline safety officials.

Conclusions

While the safety risks of federally unregulated, onshore hazardous liquid and gas gathering pipelines are generally considered to be lower than other types of pipelines, PHMSA is currently not able to determine the performance and safety of these gathering pipelines because it does not collect the necessary pipeline operator data. The agency is considering options to collect such information, which could facilitate quantitatively assessing the safety risks posed by unregulated gathering pipelines. Furthermore, these data would be critical in helping PHMSA to evaluate the sufficiency of safety regulations for gathering pipelines as required by the congressional mandate or that increasing shale development across the country might necessitate. Making data-driven, evidence-based decisions about the risks of federally unregulated gathering pipelines is especially important in a time of limited resources.

The absence of an information-sharing resource focused on federally unregulated gathering pipelines means that both states and PHMSA

---

[31]GAO, *Rail Transit: FTA Programs Are Helping Address Transit Agencies' Safety Challenges, but Improved Performance Goals and Measures Could Better Focus Efforts*, GAO-11-199 (Washington, D.C.: Jan. 31, 2011).

could miss opportunities to share lessons learned and successful practices for helping to ensure pipeline safety. Sharing such lessons and related safety reporting can help support a safety culture and increase state officials' awareness of possible safety practices or strategies that they can use to enhance pipeline safety. Lessons learned can also help states avoid the mistakes of others. Additionally, increased information sharing through such a resource would help PHMSA become more aware of state pipeline safety practices and initiatives—which in turn would assist PHMSA in sharing and supporting these safety practices, as well as in considering what state efforts may have applicability for federal programs, regulation, and guidance.

Recommendations for Executive Action

To enhance the safety of unregulated onshore hazardous liquid and gas gathering pipelines, we recommend that the Secretary of Transportation direct the PHMSA Administrator to take the following two actions:

- Collect data from operators of federally unregulated onshore hazardous liquid and gas gathering pipelines, subsequent to an analysis of the benefits and industry burdens associated with such data collection. Data collected should be comparable to what PHMSA collects annually from operators of regulated gathering pipelines (e.g., fatalities, injuries, property damage, location, mileage, size, operating pressure, maintenance history, and the causes of incidents and consequences).

- Establish an online clearinghouse or other resource for states to share information on practices that can help ensure the safety of federally unregulated onshore hazardous liquid and gas gathering pipelines. This resource could include updates on related PHMSA and industry initiatives, guidance, related PHMSA rulemakings, and other information collected or shared by states.

Agency Comments

We provided the Department of Transportation with a draft of this report for review and comment. The department provided technical corrections, which we incorporated as appropriate.

We are sending copies of this report to interested congressional committees and the Secretary of Transportation. In addition, the report is available at no charge on the GAO website at http://www.gao.gov.

If you or your staff have any questions about this report, please contact me at (202) 512-2834 or flemings@gao.gov. Contact points for our Offices of Congressional Relations and Public Affairs may be found on the last page of this report. GAO staff who made major contributions to this report are listed in appendix III.

Susan A. Fleming
Director
Physical Infrastructure Issues

Appendix I: Objectives, Scope, and Methodology

The objectives of our review were to determine (1) the safety risks that exist, if any, with onshore hazardous liquid and natural gas gathering pipelines that are not currently under the Pipeline and Hazardous Materials Safety Administration (PHMSA) regulation and (2) the practices states are using to help ensure the safety of unregulated onshore gathering pipelines. To address our objectives, we reviewed PHMSA and other federal agency regulations, as well as available safety data on regulated pipelines. We also interviewed officials at PHMSA, state pipeline safety agencies, pipeline companies and other industry stakeholders, and related associations. We obtained data on pipelines regulated by PHMSA to understand the types of pipeline data currently collected, as well as to compare and analyze accident, injury, fatality, and other trends. We reviewed the data and conducted follow-up work as necessary to determine that the data were complete, reasonable, and sufficiently reliable for the purposes of this report. We also conducted site visits—selecting locations based on geography, pipeline infrastructure, and other factors—to interview pipeline officials and representatives in Denver, Pittsburgh, and Dallas-Fort Worth. We later identified an initial list of safety risks and safety practices through information collection and document review processes.

To determine what safety risks may be associated with federally unregulated gathering pipelines—in addition to reviewing federal agency regulations, regulated pipeline safety data, and conducting various interviews—and because of the lack of historical and nationwide data, we developed and administered a web-based survey to state pipeline safety agencies in all 50 states and the District of Columbia.[1] Our survey was intended to collect information otherwise not available from PHMSA, states, industry, or other sources on safety risks associated with onshore, federally unregulated hazardous liquid and gas gathering pipelines and related safety practices to help address those risks and ensure safety. We used the survey to identify which states had unregulated, onshore gathering pipelines and what perceived pipeline safety risks were associated with those pipelines. To identify safety practices states are using, we reviewed industry documents and conducted interviews with public and private experts and officials. Then, as part of our survey of state pipeline safety agencies, we asked officials to identify the practices

---

[1]Alaska and Hawaii have chosen not to participate in pipeline arrangements with PHMSA. Therefore, a PHMSA official who conducts state pipeline safety inspections in these states responded to those states' surveys.

they used to ensure the safety of onshore, federally unregulated
hazardous liquid and gas gathering pipelines. From our survey results, we
identified the most frequently cited safety practices, including additional
state programs, activities, and other practices.

To develop the survey questions, we conducted initial interviews with
state officials and other pipeline safety stakeholders to identify safety
issues regarding unregulated gathering pipelines. We also reviewed key
literature to ascertain pipeline safety practices and other issues. We
consulted with PHMSA officials and reviewed PHMSA documentation to
identify the proper terminology for use in the survey.

The survey was pretested with potential respondents from state pipeline
safety agencies, as well as with the Congressional Research Service and
National Association of Pipeline Safety Representatives.[2] We did this to
ensure that (1) the questions were clear and unambiguous, (2) the terms
we used were precise, (3) the survey did not place an undue burden on
the agency officials completing it, and (4) the survey was independent
and unbiased. In addition, the survey was reviewed by an internal,
independent survey expert. We took steps in survey design, data
collection, and analysis to minimize nonsampling errors. For example, we
worked with PHMSA officials to identify the appropriate survey
respondents—state pipeline safety agencies. To minimize measurement
error that might occur from respondents interpreting our questions
differently from our intended purpose, we extensively pretested the
survey and followed up with nonresponding units and with units whose
responses violated certain validity checks. We identified only two cases
where the respondents had slightly varied responses from our intended
question, although the majority understood our questions as intended.
Finally, to eliminate data-processing errors, we independently verified the
computer program that generated the survey results. Our results are not
subject to sampling error because we administered our survey to all 50
state pipeline safety agencies and the District of Columbia.

The survey was conducted using self-administered electronic
questionnaires posted on the World Wide Web. We sent e-mail
notifications to 52 agencies responding to our survey. We also e-mailed

---

[2]The National Association of Pipeline Safety Representatives is a national association
representing the state pipeline safety inspectors in the contiguous United States, as well
as the District of Columbia and Puerto Rico.

each potential respondent a unique password and username to ensure
that only members of the target population could participate in the survey.
To encourage respondents to complete the survey, we sent an e-mail
reminder to each nonrespondent about 2 weeks after our initial e-mail
message. The survey data were collected from July through September
2011. We received responses from all 50 states and the District of
Columbia, for an overall response rate of 100 percent. This "collective
perspective" obtained from each of the agencies helps to mitigate
individual respondent bias by aggregating information across the range of
different viewpoints. For purposes of characterizing the results of our
survey, we identified specific meanings for the words we used to quantify
the results, as follows: "a few" means between 1 percent and 24 percent
of respondents, "some" means between 25 percent and 44 percent of
respondents, "about half" means between 45 percent and 55 percent of
respondents, "a majority" means between 56 percent and 74 percent of
respondents, "most" means between 75 percent and 94 percent of
respondents, and "nearly all" means 95 percent or more of respondents.
This report contains the central results from the survey (see app. II).

We conducted this performance audit from February 2011 to March 2012
in accordance with generally accepted government auditing standards.
Those standards require that we plan and perform the audit to obtain
sufficient, appropriate evidence to provide a reasonable basis for our
findings and conclusions based on our audit objectives. We believe that
the evidence obtained provides a reasonable basis for our findings and
conclusions based on our audit objectives.

Appendix II: Summary Results, GAO Pipeline Safety Regulations Survey

General Pipeline Safety Regulation Survey Questions	Hazardous Liquid	Natural Gas
YES RESPONSES	**Frequency**	**Frequency**
Does your state have any onshore gathering pipelines outside of high consequence areas that PHMSA does not regulate?	10	29
Does your agency collect any data for onshore gathering pipelines that PHMSA does not regulate?	4	7
Does your state have safety requirements for onshore gathering pipelines that are more stringent than those provided by PHMSA?	1	7
Subpopulation Total	**18**	**52**
How great a safety risk, if at all, are the following factors for onshore hazardous liquid and gas gathering pipelines in your state that PHMSA does not regulate?	**Hazardous Liquid**	**Natural Gas**
MODERATE AND HIGH SAFETY RISK RESPONSES	**Frequency**	**Frequency**
A. Limited or no annual reporting data (similar to PHMSA's) available on these pipelines (e.g., mileage, leaks)	1	9
B. Limited or no incident data available on these pipelines (e.g., spills, releases)	2	11
C. Limited or no information on the integrity of these pipelines[a]	2	13
D. Unknown or uncertain locations of pipelines	3	13
E. Location of these pipelines in high consequence areas[b]	4	15
F. Limited or no inspections conducted on these pipelines[a]	3	13
G. Limited or no information on the pipe size	2	7
H. Limited or no information on operating pressure[a]	3	13
I. Installation/construction quality	3	15
J. Periodic maintenance not conducted on these pipelines	3	13
K. Quality of product (sour or non-sour, corrosive, abrasive, etc.)	3	11
L. Limited information on reporting damages	2	9
M. Other (Please specify)	1	1
Subpopulation Total	**10**	**29**

[a]This response category was combined to represent an overall category of "Limited or no information of the pipeline integrity."

[b]A survey follow up found that the majority of respondents also understood the question as it was intended to mean Class 1 unregulated gathering pipelines previously located in rural areas that may have transitioned to be located in either (Class 2, 3 or 4) high consequence areas due to changing land use.

Does your agency use any of the following practices to ensure onshore hazardous liquid and gas pipeline safety in your state?	Hazardous Liquid		Natural Gas	
	Regulated Pipelines	Unregulated Gathering	Regulated Pipelines	Unregulated Gathering
YES RESPONSES	Frequency	Frequency	Frequency	Frequency
A. Considering the areas of highest risk to effectively target resources	14	3	47	7
B. Collecting and analyzing comprehensive pipeline spill/ release data on various types of pipelines	6	1	27	2
C. Standardizing spill/ release data collection in order to better assess trends or common causes of spills/ releases so that prevention measures can be targeted and evaluated to reduce future incidents	5	1	22	2
D. Engaging in outreach or other communication with communities and citizens to boost awareness or knowledge of pipelines, including their locations	10	3	37	4
E. Coordinating with operators to understand new technologies, including computer software, pipeline inspection devices, and other tools to report on pipelines	11	2	34	2
F. Using existing or emerging technologies to reduce the time required to detect pipeline leaks	8	1	21	3
G. Working to increase construction quality to ensure a long life for pipeline infrastructure	11	2	40	3
H. Prioritizing the replacement or repair of aging or otherwise limited infrastructure	9	1	37	2
I. Conducting recurring, scheduled or unscheduled safety inspections of operators	14	3	47	6
J. Establishing a system of escalated enforcement to enhance and increase regulatory attention on operators that have spills/ releases	11	2	29	4
K. Developing standards or other bench marks to measure and evaluate performance in encouraging safety	7	2	28	2
L. Monitoring implementation of corrective or preventive measures to evaluate their impact or effectiveness	13	0	40	4
M. Using existing integrity management practices for PHMSA unregulated lines	8	2	15	2
N. Implementing and enforcing a damage prevention program	13	3	38	10
O. Other (Please specify)	0	1	7	2
Subpopulation Total	**18**	**10**	**52**	**29**

Source: GAO.

Appendix III: GAO Contact and Staff Acknowledgments

GAO Contact	Susan A. Fleming, (202) 512-2834 or flemings@gao.gov
Staff Acknowledgments	In addition to the contact named above, other key contributors to this report were Sara Vermillion (Assistant Director), Matt Cail (Analyst-in-Charge), Aisha Cabrer, David Hooper, Stuart Kaufman, Josh Ormond, Jerome Sandau, Jeremy Sebest, Rebecca Shea, Don Watson, and Adam Yu.